T0067273

ACTS of the APOSTLES and ROMANS
A Devotional Bible Study

ACTS of the
APOSTLES
and ROMANS
A Devotional Bible Study

ERIC AFUM BEDIAKO

WESTBOW·
PRESS
A DIVISION OF THOMAS NELSON
& ZONDERVAN

"All Scripture quotations are taken from THE HOLY BIBLE, NEW
INTERNATIONAL VERSION®, NIV® Copyright © 1973, 1978, 1984, 2011
by Biblica, Inc.® Used by permission. All rights reserved worldwide."

WestBow Press books may be ordered through
booksellers or by contacting:

WestBow Press
A Division of Thomas Nelson & Zondervan
1663 Liberty Drive
Bloomington, IN 47403
www.westbowpress.com
1 (866) 928-1240

ISBN: 978-1-4908-7911-6 (sc)
ISBN: 978-1-4908-7913-0 (hc)
ISBN: 978-1-4908-7912-3 (e)

Library of Congress Control Number: 2015907096

Print information available on the last page.

WestBow Press rev. date: 06/10/2015

To Sylvia,

my dear wife, who through the years has
shared with me everything, including our ministry
together as Priscilla and Aquila.

CONTENTS

ACKNOWLEDGMENTS

This first attempt to put my studies into a book has mainly been supervised, edited, and encouraged by my wife, Sylvia, and my son, Ahenkora. The Rev. Dr. Theophilus B. Dankwa, Former Regional Secretary for English and Portuguese Speaking Africa, International Fellowship of Evangelical Students, supported my desire to write a devotional. Rev. Kingsley Appiagyei has allowed and encouraged me to be part of his Bible-teaching ministry at Trinity Baptist Church, London. Nana Kwame Debrah Topa (Kwamang Nifahene) has been a great encouragement to me in the Bible study classes.

INTRODUCTION

This devotional study aims to help individuals and groups study the Bible and apply it to their daily lives. The questions follow the reading of the relevant Scriptures. The aim of the notes is to help confirm and direct the reader to the main teaching of the passage.

The Acts of the Apostles outlines the work of the Holy Spirit. In this book Paul comes on the scene and faces the work he is called upon to do.

The book of Romans introduces an understanding to a balance between the law and grace. Jews and Gentiles are both justified by faith in the Lord Jesus Christ.

The Acts of the Apostles and Romans are two central books of the New Testament. The book of Acts continues the history of Jesus' followers in the period after Jesus' ascension. The book shows how God transcends men and enables them to live beyond themselves by the power of the Holy Spirit. There is a bold and dramatic movement from Jerusalem and its upper room to Rome and its prison. We see a growing group of men and women who are filled with the dynamic power of a new life. We see heroic deeds done for Christ.

The book of Romans is not a piece of casual correspondence between friends but a document. The book is the New Testament's most thorough exposition of salvation, describing its need, its nature, and its means, indicating its radical implications in the multiracial community and celebrating Jesus Christ crucified, risen, reigning, and coming as the only Savior. In Romans the universal need for salvation is set forth powerfully. The book focuses on salvation as a gift from God, through grace by the blood of Christ Jesus.

The whole human race is found guilty and inexcusable. Having been justified by faith, we enjoy peace with God, we are standing in grace, and we rejoice in the prospect of sharing God's glory (Romans 5:1–11). In Romans the fullness of both Jews and Gentiles will ultimately be gathered in (Romans 11:12, 25).

HOW TO USE THIS DEVOTIONAL

The set of questions that goes with each passage is meant to engage the reader to look for the central lessons in the sections. It is meant to help the reader devote time to Bible study and find inspiration and encouragement from the personal remarks that follow the questions.

The Bible encourages us to grow in our thinking like adults. "Brothers and sisters, stop thinking like children. In regard to evil be infants, but in your thinking be adults" (1 Corinthians 14:20). Questioning and answering is a powerful way of finding divine answers.

AUTHOR BIOGRAPHY

Eric Afum Bediako studied mathematics at the Kwame Nkrumah University of Science and Technology, Kumasi, Ghana, and later studied for the postgraduate certificate of education at the University of Cape Coast, Ghana.

In December 1976, Eric attended the Pan-African Christian Leadership Assembly (PACLA) in Nairobi, where he was challenged to undertake theological training to better understand the Bible.

He went on to study theology at the London School of Theology (LST) and the London Institute of Contemporary Christianity (LICC).

He has a passion for teaching the Bible and has led Scripture Union groups, Christian Fellowship groups and Church Adult Sunday School groups in Bible studies.

Eric is married to Sylvia and they are blessed with three sons, Angua, Ahenkora, and Afum; a daughter-in-law, Colette; and two lovely grandchildren, Olivia and Daniel Joseph.

STUDIES SECTION

Acts of the Apostles

The Book of Romans

ACTS OF THE APOSTLES

Jesus Taken Up into Heaven

Questions for Thought

1. Who wrote the book of Acts?
2. Where will the activity described in the book of Acts take place?
3. Rather than sitting around discussing the details, there is a greater job to be done. What is it?
4. Who is the Holy Spirit? What do you know already about the Holy Spirit? Where is he?
5. Did the apostles have the Holy Spirit in them when they were with Jesus?

The Acts of the Apostles can also be called "The Acts of the Holy Spirit" because it teaches about the coming and work of the Holy Spirit. Luke, the author of the book of Acts, was the Gentile physician, missionary, and traveling friend and companion of the apostle Paul.

Jesus is coming back. Looking up will not bring Him sooner. We are never told to simply stand around gazing

3

up to heaven. In fact, we are told not to do that. We are not even commanded to talk a lot about it.

Jesus will come back in the same manner as the apostles saw him go—visibly and in his glorified human body.

The gospel must first progress to Jerusalem, to Judea, and then to Samaria and "and repentance for the forgiveness of sins will be preached in his name to all nations, beginning at Jerusalem" (Luke 24:47).

The Risen Lord was first to be proclaimed where he had been slain in Jerusalem, the stronghold of his enemies. The gospel about Jesus was preached, the Holy Spirit came, and the kingdom of God was established.

The Holy Spirit Comes at Pentecost

Questions for Thought

1. How many followers were waiting in the upper room when the Holy Spirit came?
2. What is baptism "in" or "by" the Holy Spirit?
3. Is baptism in the Holy Spirit a distinct experience from the experience of being born again?
4. Are there Christians who do not have the Spirit of Christ?
5. Why do you think some of the people made fun of the disciples?

Being filled with the Holy Spirit marks the fulfillment of Jesus' predictions. Believers spoke in other tongues. "Tongues" is the ability to speak in other languages without learning them. It was supernatural and mysterious. See 1 Corinthians 12:3, Romans 8:9, and Acts 2:38.

Before Pentecost, the disciples had Jesus with them. They now had the Spirit of Christ within them at Pentecost. The Spirit is available to all who repent, believe, and are baptized into Christ.

Peter Addresses the Crowd

Questions for Thought

1. What is the difference between the work of the Holy Spirit in the Old Testament and in the New Testament?
2. God made Jesus "both Lord and Christ." What does this phrase mean?
3. What is repentance?

The work of the Holy Spirit, restricted in the Old Testament to special people, has now been enlarged to include all believers in Jesus as the Messiah. God gave the Holy Spirit to be with Jesus' church forever.

Peter announced that this man, Jesus of Nazareth, who was crucified seven weeks prior, was God's Messiah. All who responded would receive the gift of the Holy Spirit.

The resurrection of Jesus and the pouring out of the Holy Spirit both testify that Jesus is the Lord and Messiah (Romans 10:13; Luke 24:49).

The divine plan took Jesus through suffering to exaltation as Savior and Lord. The head that was once crowned with thorns is now crowned with glory. Jesus was the giver of the Spirit. He was not only Messiah but Lord. Repentance is a change of direction in a person's life rather than simply a mental change of attitude. It signifies a turning away from a sinful and godless way of life.

Peter Heals a Lame Beggar

Questions for Thought

1. What can we learn from the fact that Peter and John were going to pray while they did not have money?
2. Were Peter and John poor?
3. Peter and John told the lame beggar what they had. What did they have?
4. Do we all, as Christians, have the gift of healing?

At the hour of prayer, Peter and John came to the appointed place of public worship. Although Peter and John had no money in their pockets, they did not ignore the beggar's miserable condition. We should always do what we can to relieve the suffering of others.

The man was born with this condition; he was lame from birth. He was both poor and helpless. When God intends to save a sinner, he always uses particular means. The Lord Jesus Christ is the Almighty, all-sufficient Savior.

Christ on the tree has put away sin, and Christ on the throne is able to save.

Peter and John did have access to silver and gold; the point was that in this case they could offer something better that went to the root of the man's problem.

This incident is the first miracle of the church age. The apostles and disciples were in possession of a new power—the power of God. The new power was not for economics, politics, peace of mind, or healing, but for witnessing. It is not for a few but for everyone to possess the gift of a witness. Amen.

Ananias and Sapphira

Questions for Thought

1. What is grace?
2. What exactly was Ananias's sin?
3. In what ways do we pretend in church?
4. Who or what killed Ananias?
5. Ananias was not granted any time to repent. Why?

Both husband and wife clearly desired to contribute to the common good of the church. It was completely voluntary; they did not have to give the whole amount.

They could not have the credit of giving it all while at the same time retaining part of it. They pretended to give all of it. They hoped to gain by giving, to gain the applause of men. Their united deception amounted to a tempting or testing of the Spirit of the Lord. We are called to the service of a Holy God. See Galatians 6:7: "Do not be deceived: God cannot be mocked. A man reaps what he sows."

Ananias and Sapphira sought praise and admiration from members of the church (cf. 2 Corinthians 9:7). Hypocrisy is deliberate deception, trying to make people think we are more spiritual than we really are.

The Apostles Heal Many

Questions for Thought

1. Do signs and wonders happen today?
2. Do you have any testimonies of miracles happening today?
3. In what way should we obey God rather than men?
4. See verse 14. What do you observe about this verse?

The church is the local body of believers that possesses all the powers, rights, privileges, and prerogatives of God's redeemed children. It is also the totality of believers everywhere. The church had several new privileges, including the following:

- *New deliverance*: "But during the night an angel of the Lord opened the doors of the jail and brought them out" (Acts 5:19). It is the first deliverance of Christians by force from the power and authority of the law.

- *New authority:* Peter and the other apostles replied, "We must obey God rather than human beings!" (Acts 5:29). Gamaliel advised that if the Christian movement was merely of human origin, it would come to nothing. On the other hand, if the Christian movement has its origin in God, it will overcome human opposition. As Christians, we must be concerned about the welfare of others. Christianity is not to be a private matter.
- *A new message:* The crucifixion and resurrection of Jesus (Acts 5:30), the exaltation of Jesus (Acts 5:31), and the gift of the Holy Spirit (Acts 5:32).

Jesus Christ is the exalted Lord of glory. This Prince and Savior, the Lord Jesus Christ, is the sinner's only hope. The apostles are witnesses by the power of the Holy Spirit. Jesus' name was not a name like other names, and the Christian lifestyle was a different way of life. Amen!

STUDY 7—ACTS 6:1–15

Choosing of the Seven—
Stephen Seized

Questions for Thought

1. What were the abilities and talents of the chosen seven (i.e., the deacons)?
2. Who is a person full of the Holy Spirit?
3. What can we learn about the choosing of the seven?
4. What charges were cited against Stephen?

There was a high proportion of priests among the converts. They had acknowledged the superiority of the Christian faith. The Christian faith was not based on Judaism. We are not saved by observance of the Mosaic law but rather by faith in a resurrected Christ. God's ultimate word was to be found in Jesus, not Moses (Acts 6:14).

The apostles studied the situation and concluded that they were to blame. They were so busy serving tables that they were neglecting prayer and the ministry of the Word of God.

The apostles were all Galileans. In the eyes of men, they were a crude, uneducated rabble of fishermen and tax collectors. But Stephen was a man of learning, education, and refinement. He was a man of rank and reputation.

Stephen was accused of the following things:

- giving less importance to the centrality of the temple
- saying that Jesus would destroy the temple
- changing the whole Mosaic law

Faithfulness is one thing God requires in his service. The gospel of Christ is offensive to men, but God is faithful to his faithful servants.

Stephen's Speech to the Sanhedrin

Questions for Thought

1. What is the Christian answer to death?
2. What did Stephen preach that so angered these religious leaders?
3. Can a Christian die well?

Stephen was a Hellenist. He was full of the Holy Spirit (Acts 6:5), full of faith, full of power (Acts 6:8), and full of wisdom (Acts 6:3). Stephen is remembered as the first Christian martyr.

The process of death is the process of sleep. Death is departure or being absent in this body. It is putting off this tabernacle and going to a place prepared for us. We have a new heaven and a new earth, a city whose builder and maker is God, and a new home.

Everything in the Old Testament pointed to Christ and was fulfilled in him. Nothing takes God by surprise. Joseph was sent by God into Egypt to preserve his people. Moses was sent to deliver God's covenant people from bondage in Egypt.

Our great God can use the hands of wicked men to accomplish His purpose of grace toward his elect. The church lost Stephen, a man of great usefulness, but God had his eye on Saul, a man he would make even more useful.

He who saved Saul of Tarsus can save you. His blood is sufficient. His power is sufficient. Jesus is an able Savior.

When the time comes, God gives his believing people grace to die well. Those who die in the arms of Christ, who die in faith, die well.

Philip in Samaria /
Simon the Sorcerer

Questions for Thought

1. See verses 1–4.In what ways did Saul persecute the church?
2. How did the people know Philip's message was true?
3. Was Simon a genuine believer?
4. See verses 15 and 16.What do we learn about the baptism of the Holy Spirit?

I t took Stephen's life to open the door to the Gentiles.

Philip had no training for his missionary work. His message was on the kingdom of God and the name of Jesus. This message was confirmed to be true by miracles he performed. The result of the message was great joy in the city because their sins were blotted out, they were free from guilt, and their future was secure in Christ.

Persecution of the church in Jerusalem was turned to good effect. The disciples preached the Word as good news as they went from place to place.

Spiritual gifts cannot be gained by bribes. The Christian way is a path of humility, not of arrogance.

The Samaritans were a "half-breed" people, a mixture of Jew and Gentile. The nation originated when the Assyrians captured the ten northern tribes in 732 BC, expelled many of the people, and then introduced others who intermarried with the Jews. The Samaritans had their own temple and priesthood and openly opposed mixing with the Jews (John 4:9).

Philip and the Ethiopian Eunuch

Questions for Thought

1. What do we learn about evangelism here?
2. Is it possible to be reading the Scriptures with enthusiasm but with no understanding? (See 2 Timothy 4:3-4)
3. What is the way of salvation?
4. Are there any testimonies in your life to confirm God's perfect timings?

Philip was not told or even given a hint of the real and important nature of the assignment.

A eunuch normally is a person who has been castrated. Such people were forbidden entry to the temple by the Jewish law (Deuteronomy 23:1).

The Ethiopian was led to faith by realizing that the prophecies in the Old Testament are fulfilled in Jesus Christ. God intervenes in the lives of groups of people and individuals alike.

God moves in mysterious ways, his wonders to perform. His timings are perfect. The crossing of Philip's and the Eunuch's paths was no coincidence. It was all in the plan of God.

Philip the deacon became the interpreter of Scripture, an evangelist, and the baptizer of a new convert.

Praise the Lord!

Saul's Conversion

Questions for Thought

1. Was Saul spiritually blind?
2. Was Ananias right in complaining after seeing such a vision?
3. What do we learn about Saul's conversion?
4. See Romans 8:16.What proves that one is born again?

God arrested Saul. God was continuing to work out his plan to bring the gospel to the whole world. On the Damascus road, Saul's spiritual eyes were opened but his physical eyes were closed.

We should never be afraid to obey God's will. When God commands, we should remember that he is working "at both ends of the line" and that his perfect will is always the best. We must never underestimate the value of one person brought to Christ.

Saul was witness to the saving grace of Jesus Christ. He saw himself for what he really was in the eyes of God.

Ananias furiously questioned his guidance. Surely something had to be wrong with the vision. The reputation and the authority Saul had were sufficient to put fear into most men.

But God can annul everything so his purpose can be achieved. Ananias needed a lot of courage. The Damascus disciples are to be commended for the way in which they at once received the converted persecutor. The Jerusalem church was afraid of Saul.

God's choices fall on many unexpected people.

Saul in Damascus and Jerusalem

Questions for Thought

1. Why did Saul go to Arabia?
2. Saul preached that Jesus is the Son of God. What does it mean?
3. What did Saul do when he was with Peter in Jerusalem?
4. Why do Christians suffer?
5. What should you do if your testimony is not accepted?

It is likely that Saul's visit to Arabia took place when he fled from Damascus. The important thing about this Arabian trip is the fact that Saul did not "consult any human being" after he had received his message and mandate directly from the Lord (Galatians 1:16-17).

Paul at once recognized that Jesus was no mere man. He soon came to the conclusion that Jesus was not only the Son of God but was also the long-awaited Messiah.

Paul's preaching began with the assertion that Jesus is the Son of God, who has fulfilled the Old Testament messianic prophecies. Paul stood alone between two religious bodies, Judaism and Christianity, for neither accepted him (Habakkuk 3:17–19).

Peter at Cornelius' House/ Peter Explains His Actions

Questions for Thought

1. What is the greatest miracle God can do for us?
2. Does what happened in Cornelius's house suggest that every new believer speaks in tongues to give evidence that he or she has received the gift of the Holy Spirit?
3. What is the place of water baptism when we first believe in Jesus Christ?

The greatest miracle is salvation because its cost is the greatest. It produces the greatest results, and it brings the greatest glory to God. Salvation is a divine work of grace, but God works through human channels.

Philip was already in Caesarea, but God sent Peter, who was thirty miles away in Joppa. God works at the right time and also through the right servant. The three men from

Caesarea arrived at the door just as Peter was pondering the meaning of the vision.

Wherever there is a searching heart, God responds. The Holy Spirit was giving witness to the six Jews who were present that the Gentiles were truly born again.

The Gentiles were not saved by being baptized; they were baptized because they gave evidence of having been saved.

Sinners are always saved by faith. Hallelujah!

The Church in Antioch

Questions for Thought

1. How did Barnabas encourage these new Gentile believers?
2. Why did Barnabas go so far to Tarsus to find Paul as his assistant?
3. What sort of help did the Jewish believers receive from the Gentiles?
4. What does it mean to become a member of a church?

Antioch was the capital of Syria, three hundred miles from Jerusalem. Antioch was a wicked city, perhaps second only to Corinth. The local shrine was dedicated to Daphne, whose worship included immoral practices.

The elders commissioned Barnabas to go to Antioch to find out what was going on among the Gentiles. He rejoiced at what he saw. What was happening was the work of God, and Barnabas gave thanks for God's grace.

Saul had been converted for ten years when Barnabas brought him to Antioch. The church in Antioch is a splendid example of how we as believers ought to show gratitude in a practical way to those who have helped us in our Christian lives.

Members of the church were believers in the gospel. They were baptized believers. When a pagan became a Christian, he immediately separated himself from all contact with paganism so he could maintain his witness without compromise.

Peter's Miraculous Escape from Prison

Questions for Thought

1. Why did God allow James to die while Peter was rescued?
2. What gave Peter such confidence and peace in prison so that the angel even had to wake him from sleep while he was chained to two soldiers (John 21:18–19)?
3. What do we learn from Acts 12:5 about a praying church?
4. Were the praying Christians full of unbelief when God answered their prayers before they could say the last amen?

God permitted Herod to arrest Peter and put him under heavy guard in prison. Sixteen soldiers, four for each watch, kept guard over the apostle, with two soldiers chained to the prisoner and two watching the doors.

God allowed Herod to kill James, but God kept him from harming Peter. It was the throne in heaven that was in control, not the throne on earth.

In Jesus, Old Testament prophecies have been fulfilled. Jesus was born of the seed of David. Jesus died according to the Scriptures to deliver man from this present age. Jesus was buried. He rose again on the third day, according to the Scriptures. He has been exalted as Son of God and as Lord of the living and the dead. He will return as Judge and Savior (1 Peter 3:12).

Barnabas and Saul Sent Off

Questions for Thought

1. See verse 43. What does it mean to continue in the grace of God?
2. How can we accept somebody as different (Acts 15:38)?
3. What do you learn from verse 41?
4. How were the apostles attacked in verse 50?

Until now Jerusalem had been the center of ministry, and Peter had been the key apostle. But from this point on, Antioch in Syria would become the new center (Acts11:19ff), and Paul the new leader. The gospel was on the move. Paul and Barnabas went off by the Spirit to no specific place.

The proconsul believed after Paul demonstrated God's power on Elymas the sorcerer. Christianity was powerful enough to affect even the highest ranks of society.

This is what Paul preached: God had established his people and through the ancestral line of David Jesus had been born. He placed the responsibility for the death of Jesus on the Jerusalem Jews. Christ is superior to David by the resurrection. There is forgiveness of sins through Christ for all who believe, which exceeds anything the law of Moses could offer. There is justification through Christ, not Moses. There was an equality of salvation for Jews and Gentiles.

No wonder the Gentiles were glad as they listened to the message.

Two Faithful Gospel Preachers—Paul and Barnabas

Questions for Thought

1. What is the purpose or place of miracles in evangelism?
2. Were the apostles being cowards by fleeing?
3. What did Paul and Barnabas preach?
4. What happened when Paul and Barnabas preached Christ crucified?

The apostles did not accept the honor and use it as a basis to preach the gospel. The apostles did not want to risk death in Iconium, but they left behind a thriving community.

The faith of Paul was remarkable; he did not speak softly. Everyone in the area heard him. It was clearly a special instance of divine healing. The apostles, immediately knowing the danger, tore their garments as sign of their humble position.

Paul was evidently hit and dragged out of the city to be left as dead. Barnabas seems to have escaped. Some Christians rushed to assist Paul, who came around sufficiently to accompany Barnabas to Derbe. He tasted some of the medicine given to Stephen, but God had other work for him yet to do.

Paul and Barnabas preached the gospel, Christ crucified, the glory of his person as the *God-man* mediator, and his work as standing in for sinners and as ruler of the whole world. The preaching of Christ crucified tripped up the Jews and it was foolishness to the Gentiles, but to those who are called by God, those who are saved by God's grace, Christ crucified is the wisdom of God revealed and the power of God experienced in their souls (1 Corinthians 1:23–24, Isaiah 59:1–2).

Do Not Close the Doors

Questions for Thought

1. What is the place of the law in the Christian life?
2. What were these legalists actually doing, and why were they so unhealthy?
3. Are there modern-day Christian conditions we place on people in addition to having faith in Jesus?
4. What does this mean: "it is through the grace of our Lord Jesus that we are saved." (Acts 15:11)?

Some teachers taught that the Gentiles, in order to be saved, had to be circumcised and obey the law of Moses. They were saying, "Gentiles must become Jews before they can become Christians. It is not sufficient for them simply to trust Jesus Christ. They must also obey Moses." Salvation is wholly by God's grace through faith in Christ, plus nothing else.

Peter made it clear to the council that God made him preach the gospel to the Gentiles, that God gave the Holy Spirit to the Gentiles, and that God erased the difference between Jews and Gentiles. Jews and Gentiles are all sinners before God and can be saved only by faith in Jesus Christ. Circumcision and its implications were an unbearable yoke.

There is freedom in the gospel. God was acting in a big way on behalf of the Gentiles. When God acts, highly prized traditions may have to be modified or even scrapped.

Paul and Silas in Prison

Questions for Thought

1. Why did Paul make Timothy get circumcised while Titus was not forced to be circumcised (Acts 16:3) (Galatians 2:3)?
2. How can one be sensitive to the leading of the Holy Spirit?
3. What do we learn from Lydia's character and the role of women in God's kingdom?
4. Could evil spirits speak the truth?

Timothy's circumcision was a matter of convenience. If Timothy remained uncircumcised, it would be a hindrance when Paul was working among the Jews. The Holy Spirit closes doors as well as open doors.

Lydia was a businesswoman who traded in the famous purple dyes of her home district. God can do great things in Christian households, and in the case of Lydia, there was an immediate offer of kindness for the missionaries.

In prison Paul and Silas had their minds concentrated on prayer. The more they prayed, the more the Spirit of praise filled their minds. They began to sing freely. Other prisoners were surprised enough to listen.

Earthquakes can be a frightening experience. The moment the jailer believed in Christ, it took no time before he dressed their wounds even before he asked to be baptized. In addition, after the baptism, he gave them food. This incident shows that the gospel can change people. Where fear and confusion abound, the gospel brings peace.

Paul and Silas in Thessalonica, Berea, and Athens

Questions for Thought

1. See verse 4.Which famous Christian ladies come to mind in the early church life (Romans 16)?
2. How can we help our Christian ladies serve the Lord better in present-day church life?
3. See verse 3. What was Paul's method of preaching?
4. What is worldliness, and how has the world affected the present-day church?

Christian ladies played an important part in early church life. Examples are Priscilla, Phoebe, Lydia, Mary, Tryphena, Tryphosa, Persis, Rufus' mother, other sisters, and Nereus' sister (Romans 16). As reflected from the Berean Christians, we are encouraged to study the Scriptures for ourselves.

The church now walks hand in hand with the world and has married the world. Instead of setting the world on fire with the truth of God, the church warms itself with the fires of the world, fires powered by burning God's truth.

The church today has betrayed Christ, betrayed the souls of men, and betrayed the gospel of the grace of God. All has been sold for the silver of praise, popularity, and worldly recognition. The Christian gospel is the gospel of faith in Christ for salvation: of repentance from sin and of judgment for sin.

God controls the futures of people and nations as well as individuals. Paul speaks of the majesty of God and God's closeness to every individual. Repentance involves a major change of mind, not merely an academic adjustment.

Paul, Silas, and Timothy in Corinth

Questions for Thought

1. What does it mean to preach that Jesus is the Christ?
2. See verse 6. How long should we continue to spend time on people who abuse and slander us when we witness to them?
3. See verses 9 and 10. Has the Lord encouraged you before in the face of difficulties?

Corinth was noted for its temple of Aphrodite, where the cult of Astarte practiced its immoral rituals.

To preach there was a difficult task, but Paul found two companions: Aquila and his wife, Priscilla. They had the same trade as Paul; they were tentmakers. At this point Silas and Timothy arrived from Macedonia.

God's power was great enough to win many believers even in the most shameful city in Greece. In general, Paul made it his duty just to preach the gospel. Whether they accepted it or not was not his responsibility.

Ephesus was the most important city in the province of Asia. It was the center of the worship of Artemis, whose temple was its special pride.

Apollos was aware only of John's baptism and had received an insufficient account of Christian teaching. Priscilla and Aquila gave him a more complete teaching of Christianity (2 Corinthians 4:7; Matthew 7:6).

Paul in Ephesus

Questions for Thought

1. How did Paul know that the believers at Ephesus had not received the Holy Spirit?
2. How do we know today that someone has received the Holy Spirit?
3. What do we notice about Paul's approach to preaching or evangelizing?
4. Do we see showdowns today of counterfeit preachers like what happened to the sons of Sceva?

When Paul laid his hands on the Ephesians they also received the gift of the Holy Spirit.

During his ministry in the hall of Tyrannus, Paul was used by God to perform miracles. Just as people were healed through Peter's shadow falling upon them, so with Paul healing flowed through handkerchiefs and aprons he had touched. The healing was not only from physical ailments but also from demonic possession.

Paul had learned to withdraw from the synagogue at Jewish opposition. He found another hall (Hall of Tyrannus) and used it probably in the afternoons for two years. Luke, the author of Acts, says in Acts 19:10 that all Asia heard the word of the Lord during this period.

What happened to the sons of Sceva is a powerful demonstration that God would allow no counterfeit to his working. Through it all, the name of Jesus was lifted up.

The public burning of the magical books testifies in a powerful way to the worthlessness of the magical spells.

Riot at Ephesus

Questions for Thought

1. Should we listen to advice from Christian friends when God is leading us in a different direction?
2. Was Paul prevented from preaching the gospel to the mob by his friends and fellow Christians?
3. See verse 37. Did Paul and his companions attack the goddess Artemis?
4. To what extent can economic interest creep into true Christian devotion?

Demetrius, a silversmith, organized a protest based on the damage the gospel was doing to his trade and therefore his wealth. The bank balances of these men were more important than the people being delivered from demons and being born again.

Gaius and Aristarchus were Europeans who had apparently joined Paul in Macedonia. Paul and his friends did not make any direct attack on the goddess. It was an indirect approach that had been so effective in undermining her influence. When the truth was proclaimed, error at once diminished.

Christianity is unique in its revelation of God through Jesus Christ. "So in Christ Jesus you are all children of God through faith" (Galatians 3:26) When true Christian devotion comes into conflict with the economic interests of religion, anger is aroused and trouble is afoot. Christianity is in conflict with religious practices. It is opposed to and at war with religion in its many forms.

The center of the gospel is Jesus Christ. He is the fulfillment of the Old Testament prophecies, born of the Seed of David, died for our sins, was buried, was raised, and will come as Judge and King. Our aim for preaching the gospel is love, not anger, and the glory of God, not the praise of men.

A Minister's Farewell

Questions for Thought

1. See verse 24.What does Paul mean by saying his life is worth nothing unless he uses it for God's work?
2. See verse 26.Why does Paul say that if any of them died spiritually it was not his fault?
3. See verses 31–35.What warnings are we given here about carelessness, superficiality and hollowness, covetousness, envy and jealousy, laziness and idleness, selfishness, self-centeredness, and self-interest?

Paul determined to finish his course with joy, no matter what the cost might be. Paul told sinners to repent of their sins and believe in Jesus Christ. He declared to them "the whole will of God" (Acts 20:27b)

It is the nature of the gospel to arouse opposition, and Paul had come to terms with this. His concern was more for the faithful completion of his ministry than for his own safety. People with influence can undermine and lead others astray. Paul reminded them of his tears on their behalf. The farewell was particularly moving. The whole company—the elders and members of Paul's party—knelt and prayed as Paul led them. There was not a dry eye (2 Corinthians 11:24–27).

The Misunderstood Missionary

Questions for Thought

1. See verse 13. Is it a good Christian attitude to look forward to dying for the sake of the Lord Jesus Christ?
2. Paul listened to the plea of Christians during the riot in Athens, but he could not be stopped from going to Jerusalem. Why?
3. Should one put personal safety before devotion to one's calling?
4. See verse 21.What were Paul's enemies saying about him?

God's people may suggest what other people's leading should be, only to find that the others do not share the same convictions. Philip's house was certainly an unusual household with all four daughters devoted to prophetic ministry.

Agabus (11:27–30) was a notable Jerusalem prophet who had already made a startling announcement at Antioch regarding the coming famine and had inspired the church there to send relief to the Judean Christians. Paul's desire was to fulfill his mission in the name of Jesus. If that meant captivity or even death in Jerusalem, it could not deflect him.

The Jerusalem Christians rejoiced over God's activity among the Gentiles, but there were many Jewish Christians who had other views of Paul's activity. A report was circulating that he was urging Jewish Christians to forsake Moses. Some Christians believed this and circulated false reports.

Paul Is Arrested

Questions for Thought

1. What does it mean to be saved?
2. Are there present-day equivalents of bringing Gentiles to the temple?
3. How did Paul make use of his Roman citizenship for the cause of Christ?
4. Was it out of pride that Paul was giving all these pre-Christian credentials?

In the temple, separating the court of the Gentiles from the other courts stood a wall beyond which by law no Gentile was allowed to go to. The Romans had granted the Jewish religious leaders authority to deal with anybody who broke this law. No devout Jew would have anything to do with the Gentiles.

Paul was accused of being seen in the city with a Gentile Trophimus. He was seen with other men in the temple, and they had concluded that he had taken a Gentile into the temple. The whole city was in chaos, and Paul was dragged from the temple. It was a riot with a strong religious motive, the worst kind of acts of inhumanity. Paul sustained blows and beatings until the army intervened and formally arrested him.

Paul preferred to be a prisoner than give up his burden for lost souls and for missions. Paul was a Jew who was educated in Jerusalem under no less a teacher than Gamaliel, had a zeal for the law, and persecuted those who belonged to "the Way."

As soon as Paul realized he was going to be interrogated by scourging, he announced his Roman citizenship. Such citizenship protected a man from scourging and in fact required a proper trial before punishment. God protected Paul and eventually got him to Rome, and the Romans paid the bill.

Paul the Prisoner

Questions for Thought

1. What is conscience?
2. Why did Paul cause confusion between the Pharisees and Sadducees?
3. Was Paul a failure in Jerusalem?

Paul was under military protection, which meant he was bound to a Roman soldier who was responsible for him.

Conscience is the inner "judge" or "witness" that approves when we do right and disapproves when we do wrong (Romans 2:15).

Paul realized he could never get a fair trial before the Sanhedrin, so the wisest thing was to end the hearing as soon as possible and trust God to use the Roman legions to protect him from the Jews. The real issue was Jesus Christ and the resurrection.

Paul's Jerusalem journey led to riot in the temple and confusion in the Sanhedrin, but the Lord was pleased with Paul. "Take courage! As you have testified about me in Jerusalem, so you must also testify in Rome" (Acts 23:11b).

God arranged for 470 Roman soldiers to protect Paul and take him to Caesarea. Paul did not look for the easy way but for the way that would most honor the Lord and win the lost. He was even willing to become a prisoner if that would further the work of the gospel.

Paul was alone—but not alone.

When Is It the Best
Time to be Saved?

Questions for Thought

1. See verse 21.How important is the church's witness
    to the resurrection of Jesus Christ (Acts 1:22)?
2. See verse 25.What is righteousness, self-control,
    and the judgment to come in Christianity?
3. How does one repent and believe on Jesus Christ?
4. See verse 25.When is the best time to be saved?

Paul was accused of being a "ringleader of the sect of
the Nazarenes." Satan's most powerful weapon is to
convince us not to hurry. The best time to trust Jesus
Christ is *now*. And the best time to tell others the good
news of the gospel is *now*.

Time is short and uncertain, can never be reversed, and
can never be changed. Clocks tell us what time it is, but

the Bible tells us what to do with time. *The best time to be saved is when the gospel is first heard.*

Christianity upsets people because it uncovers sin. It offends intelligence because it can only be known by revelation, and it offends because it declares one's righteousness to be like filthy rags.

The Bible alone is the Word of God. God Almighty, Father, Son, and Holy Spirit, is sovereign. All men and women are sinners, and the Lord chose a people before the world began and redeemed all God's elect by grace and faith to eternal salvation.

Amen!

Warning: Read Proverbs 1:24–26.

Paul the Defender

Questions for Thought

1. Do you have a task God has given you that makes you sure nothing can stop you, even death?
2. Does Satan's wicked intention stop after the passing of time?
3. What is the Gospel?
4. See Acts 26:28. How long does it usually take to become a Christian?

Paul was a Jew whose countrymen wanted to kill him, and he was a Roman whose government did not know what to do with him.

Paul affirmed that he was innocent of any crime against the Jewish law, the temple, or the Roman government. Paul knew his destination was Rome, not Jerusalem, and that the fastest way to get there was to appeal to Caesar. He knew the Jews had not given up their hope of killing him and that he could never have a fair trial in Jerusalem.

Paul was declaring and defending the resurrection of Jesus Christ. His key statements were that He lived as a Pharisee, saw a light, heard a voice, was not disobedient, and had continued to this day witnessing about what happened to him.

It was because of his convictions about the resurrection and "the hope of Israel" that he was a prisoner. God offers his covenant blessings to both Jews and Gentiles on the same terms of repentance and faith.

It is a wonderful thing to have an opportunity to trust Jesus Christ and be saved. And it is a terrible thing to waste that opportunity and perhaps never have another.

The Shipwreck

Questions for Thought

1. Has the Lord encouraged you in a difficult situation before?
2. What part can "storms" play in the Christian's life?
3. What is the secret behind Paul's extraordinary coolness, authority, and foresight?
4. Is life necessarily smooth sailing when you are in the will of God?

Paul said in Acts19:21b, "I must visit Rome also." But before then there was an illegal arrest, Roman and Jewish trials, and confinement and shipwreck. Paul was a courageous leader who could take command of a difficult situation in a time of great crisis. Paul began as a prisoner in the ship but ended as the captain of the ship.

There are times when one dedicated believer can change the whole atmosphere of a situation simply by trusting God and making that faith visible. Even the worst storms cannot hide the face of God or hinder the purposes of

God. Storms can give us opportunities to serve others and bear witness to Jesus Christ. Paul was the most valuable man on that ship. He knew how to pray, he had faith in God, and he was in touch with the Almighty.

Paul was forced to endure three things: (1) troubles, despair, hunted down, being knocked down, etc. (2 Corinthians 4:7–11); (2) imprisonment, sleepless nights, slander, poverty, etc. (2 Corinthians 6:4–10); and (3) facing death again and again, beatings, facing dangers from rivers and robbers, having a burden for all the churches, etc. (2 Corinthians 11:23–30).

Paul was a man of courage and faith.

Paul Arrives in Rome

Questions for Thought

1. Was the viper a weapon of Satan to get Paul out of the way?
2. How did the gospel ever get from the Jews in Jerusalem to the Gentiles in Rome?
3. What is a successful life, and what is the triumph of a well-lived life?

The shipwrecked people after the ordeal found themselves on a friendly island of Malta. Once again the apostle Paul is seen to be under a divine protection, in keeping with his assurance that he must stand before Caesar.

Paul's greatest concern was his witness to the Jews in Rome. He made it clear that he was a prisoner "on behalf" of his nation and "the hope of Israel." During the following two years, Paul wrote Philippians, Ephesians, Colossians, and Philemon. Many believe he was released and traveled as far as Spain.

He was arrested again, and this time he was chained in prison and treated like a criminal. Second Timothy 1:16 and 2:9 say Paul knew that the end was coming (2 Timothy 4:6–8). Tradition tells us that he was beheaded at Rome in AD 67/68. Paul was a man of faith but also of works. He was a man of prayer but also of action. Christianity is life and experience, contest and conquest, trial and triumph.

Learn to trust God's providence (Genesis 50:20; Romans 8:28). Learn to do what God has given you the ability and opportunity to do for the glory of Christ and the good of immortal souls (Ecclesiastes 9:10). Learn that all who honor God will be honored by God (1 Samuel 2:30).

ROMANS

The Unashamed Man

Questions for Thought

1. Who were the apostles?
2. From Romans16:1–2, what do we learn about Phoebe?
3. Who founded the church in Rome?
4. What is faith that leads to salvation?
5. What is the gospel?
6. See verse 17. "The righteous will live by faith." What does it mean?

Paul wrote this letter in AD 58. At that time he was the houseguest of a man named Gaius (Romans 16:23), a wealthy citizen of the Grecian city of Corinth. Phoebe (Romans 16:1), a widow of considerable wealth who served as a deaconess in the Christian church of Cenchrea, took Paul's letter to Rome.

Phoebe became the postwoman God used. She probably did not know the importance of the document she was carrying. It is indeed a tribute to women that so important a document and so sacred a trust should have been put into the hands of a woman.

The Christian life begins in faith and continues in faith. It was born by faith, and it lives by faith.

The gospel is not good advice to be followed. It is a divinely given message concerning a divine person, the Son of God, Jesus Christ our Lord. It is a declaration of who Jesus is and through whom men can be put right with God. It is the climax and fulfillment of what God had long promised through His prophets.

Paul's whole life from the time of his conversion was dedicated to the faith he once tried to destroy. Every qualification of an apostle was found in Paul.

The Inexcusable Man

Questions for Thought

1. What is this righteousness that is revealed in the gospel?
2. See verses 17–20.Why is the man who has not heard the gospel without excuse?
3. Where is the meeting place now between God and man?
4. See verse 26. Has God abandoned men and women today to their shameful desires?

Man needs a righteousness that will make him right with God. The means of such righteousness is the gospel. Man has no excuse because the righteousness of God is revealed in the gospel (Romans 1:17).

The righteousness is the person of Jesus Christ. We are to follow him. Man has no excuse because the wrath of God is revealed from heaven (Romans 1:18). Man has no excuse because the knowledge of God is revealed in nature (Romans 1:19–20).

The highest revelation of God is in Jesus, and in him is the righteousness of God. What man has tried to regain by religious achievement through the law, through works, and through worship is really gained by faith, for "the righteous will live by faith" (Romans 1:17b). The opposite of works is the righteousness of God. When we receive this righteousness of God by faith, we are fulfilling the law.

Our bodies are now intended to be God's meeting place with man. The last bulwark of any civilization is its womanhood (Romans 1:26). Undesirable sexual relationships were common then as they are now.

The Judgment

Questions for Thought

1. What is judgment? Are we ever permitted to judge others (1 Corinthians 11:31, 5:12–13)?
2. What advice would you give someone who has been judged and maliciously criticized?
3. What is the Golden Rule (Luke 6:27–31)?
4. See verse 15. What is the fate of those who do not have the Law and have not heard the gospel?
5. See verse 11. Does God sometimes show favoritism to some people?

There is a tendency in us to condemn others and excuse ourselves. There is but one time we are permitted to sit in judgment—when we judge ourselves (1 Corinthians 11:31).

If you worry about what people think of you, it means you have more confidence in their opinions than in your own. God wipes our pasts with his grace (1 Timothy 5:24).

Our entrance into heaven is gained through the possession of the life of Jesus Christ. The law has been a standard and not a salvation. A man is to be judged on the basis of what light he has. The Israelites were judged by the Law and were only accepted before God through the altars of sacrifice.

For all who live outside revealed Christianity, there are two sources of light. The first is the light of nature in which the judge is experience, and the second is the light of reason in which the judge is one's conscience.

The law never gave life; it is only in Jesus that there is life. Jews and Gentiles are essentially on the same footing before God. There is no favoritism in God's court.

The True Jew

Questions for Thought

1. Who is a Christian?
2. What is the power in Christianity?
3. Is it possible to be a serious Christian within but show no outward evidence?
4. See verses 28–29.Who is a true Jew?

Christianity is the possession of a life. A Christian is a spiritual organism that carries out the functions of a spiritual life.

Words are not enough to affirm one's commitment to Christ. It requires works to support words. The Jews took refuge in the law of Moses, but protection was not in having the Law but in keeping it.

The instructor in spiritual things is required to possess a practice equivalent to his teaching. The message is measured by the messenger (2 Timothy 3:5).

Christianity is a force of divine power. The greatest evidence of a true gospel is a pure life proceeding from that gospel. Sometimes we do not have sufficient inward life to meet the outward testing.

God's patience does not tolerate inconsistency but gives opportunity for repentance. The Jews placed too much stress on circumcision. It is better to be uncircumcised and keep the law than be circumcised and not keep it.

God Remains Faithful

Questions for Thought

1. Do the Jews have an advantage over the Gentiles (John 4:22)?
2. Is there any advantage in just being a church-goer?
3. Can you get good out of evil?
4. See verse 20. What is the purpose of the Law?

The Jews had an inheritance. They were the custodians of God's revelation in the past. Even if the Jews failed God, He would never fail them. They have every right to be known as "the people of God." God will not exempt them from judgment so they do not have any special favors as such.

Decency and honesty are the hallmarks of Christianity. Sin affects every part of our human constitution, every faculty and function, including our minds, emotions, sexuality, consciences, and wills.

The reason the Law cannot justify sinners is precisely because its function is to expose and to condemn their sin (Romans 3:20b). And the reason the law condemns us is because we break it. What the law brings is the knowledge of sin, not forgiveness of sin.

People are a mess, and there is nothing we can do to put it right. God is certainly going to judge us. The only hope for us is that there should be offered to us a righteousness outside ourselves, which could become ours by being credited to our account. And the good news is that such righteousness is offered (Romans 3:21–22). "This righteousness is given through faith in Jesus Christ to all who believe." Amen!

The One Way of Salvation

Questions for Thought

1. What is the one way of salvation revealed in the gospel?
2. What does it mean to be declared righteous?
3. Is there any difference between being pardoned and being justified?
4. If salvation comes by faith, does it mean you don't do anything to be saved?
5. How is the Law fulfilled in Christ?

Pardon will say, "You may go; you have been let off the penalty which your sin deserves." *Justification* (verdict that means acceptance) will say, "You may come; you are welcome to all my love and my presence." Pardon is the remission of punishment, and justification is a declaration that there are no grounds for infliction of punishment.

Every justified believer has also been regenerated by the Holy Spirit and so put on the road to progressive holiness.

The saving initiative from beginning to end belongs to God the Father. Through the cross of Christ, God has redeemed his people.

The Jews' privileges were not intended for the exclusion of the Gentiles but for their ultimate inclusion. Through Abraham's posterity, "all people on earth" would be blessed. The covenant with Abraham has been fulfilled in Christ.

Faith is taking God at his word.

New Life in Christ

Questions for Thought

1. There is only one way of salvation. What is it?
2. Do you have to do anything to contribute to your salvation?
3. What was the purpose of Abraham's circumcision?
4. What does it mean to believe? What is faith?
5. What is the seal, pledge, or guarantee from God that we have become Christians (Ephesians 1:13–14)?

The Old Testament saints were saved in exactly the same way as we are (Ephesians 2:11–22). There is only one gospel. There is only one way of salvation.

Abraham was declared righteous before he was circumcised. God credits faith as righteousness. This is not a rewarding of merit but a free and unmerited decision of divine grace.

Abraham received the sign of circumcision as a seal of the righteousness that he had by faith while he was still uncircumcised. Abraham is the father of all believers, irrespective of whether they are circumcised or uncircumcised. Where circumcision divides, faith unites.

Justification does not make us righteous; it declares us to be righteous because the righteousness of Jesus Christ is put to our account. Faith consists of accepting what God has said, not fulfilling what God has demanded. Abraham never saw the fulfillment of the promise. He died believing that God would keep his word (Hebrews 11:13).

The believer is sealed with the Holy Spirit of promise, which is the earnest (pledge money) of our inheritance (a guarantee) until the redemption of the purchased possession.

The Justified Man/ Abraham's Faith

Questions for Thought

1. Has man a bit of righteousness of his own?
2. Who started the plan of redemption?
3. What is justification?
4. Why is Abraham the father of all believers?
5. What is the grace of God?

Man has no righteousness of his own. God's righteousness is available for all who believe in Christ. Redemption has been initiated by God and so there is no room for boasting or pride.

Abraham's justification was on the basis of his faith (Genesis 15:5–6). His act of faith was before he was circumcised. Because of this Abraham could be the father of all believers, whether circumcised or uncircumcised.

Faith always looks at problems in the light of the promises of God.

The Christian faith stands on what God did when he raised Jesus from the dead. God is gracious. Grace gives and faith takes. Faith's function is humbly to receive what grace offers. Only the gospel of grace and faith can unite Jews and Gentiles, by opening the door to the Gentiles and leveling everybody at the foot of Christ's cross (Romans 3:29). This is God's way of salvation for everybody (Romans 4:25).

Do not simply wait. Work. Do not merely believe something. Do something. Do not merely say something. Be someone!

The Results of Justification

Questions for Thought

1. What are some of the results of our being justified before God?
2. How does suffering help build character?
3. What do we learn about the nature of God's love?
4. What is the proof that God loves us?
5. Are we half-saved, and do we look forward to full salvation?

Because of what Jesus has done, God will not hold our sins against us. God's love in sending Christ to die for us happened while we were sinners. To escape God's wrath is marvelous for the sinner, but to be reconciled, to have restored relationships as if sin had never happened, is more marvelous still.

Suffering is the one and only path to glory. It was for Christ; it is also for Christians.

The Holy Spirit is God's gift to all believers, so it is not possible to be justified by faith without at the same time being regenerated and indwelt by the Holy Spirit (Romans 5:5). The Holy Spirit pours God's love into our hearts.

Salvation began at the cross and will be completed at the throne. We were saved by Christ, the Lamb of God, dying. We are kept saved by Christ, the High Priest of God, living. We do not wait for the outpouring of God's wrath, but we are looking forward to the unveiling of his glory.

If God did such good to us when we were sinners and enemies, it is certain that he will do even more good to us now that we are his friends. If Christ's death secured our reconciliation, how much more shall his life secure our final salvation!

Adam and Christ Contrasted

Questions for Thought

1. How can it be said that all people born into the world sinned in Adam?
2. Is it fair that the righteousness of Christ should be imputed on me?
3. Do you believe salvation reaches all people?
4. Is there a limit to the grace of God?
5. What was the objective or purpose of God in giving the Law at all?

Being "in Adam" describes the prison house of sin. Adam sinned, so we all sinned. Adam's sin and its results were passed on to us. Christ's obedience and righteousness are passed on to all who believe in him.

God justifies the ungodly. It is a free gift. If you are relying upon the fact that you believe, you are ruining it. It is entirely the free gift of God's grace. God no longer looks at you as a sinner. You are not a sinner; you are a child of

God. Grace forgives sin through the cross and bestows on the sinner both righteousness and eternal life.

Until the law, sin was in the world, and death reigned from Adam to Moses. The law increases our knowledge of sin. It brings out the awful deceitfulness of sin.

Grace satisfies the thirsty soul and fills the hungry with good things. Grace sanctifies sinners, shaping them into the image of Christ. One day grace will destroy death and usher us into the kingdom of God.

God's throne is a throne of grace. Sin may be the king in the region dominated by death, but grace occupies the throne in the realm of eternal life.

Dead to Sin, Alive in Christ

Questions for Thought

1. Do we sometimes feel free to sin because we are under grace and God will forgive us?
2. What does it mean to be dead to sin and alive to God?
3. How can sin be our master?
4. Do Christians who have died to sin commit sin?

Having formerly belonged to Adam, the author of sin and death, we now belong to Christ, the author of salvation and life. Although at one point in the history of Israel the law was added to increase sin, grace increased all the more so that grace might reign. "The law was brought in so that trespass might increase. But where sin increased, grace increased all the more, so that, just as sin reigned in death, so also grace might reign through righteousness to bring eternal life through Jesus Christ our Lord" (Romans 5:20–21).

God's grace not only forgives sin but also delivers us from sinning, for grace does more than justify; it also sanctifies. Does grace undermine ethical responsibility and promote reckless sinning? The response is, "By no means!" (Romans 6:2, 15), certainly not! If we ask this question then we have not understood the meaning of our conversion and baptism.

To die to sin is to become insensitive to it. We should be unresponsive to temptation as a corpse is to a physical stimulus. Passion is not necessarily wrong, but obeying passion is wrong. The Christian has a new standard of teaching and has no option but to obey it. He will be sanctified as he obeys the new standard of teaching.

Since we have died to sin, it is inconceivable that we should let sin reign in us or ourselves to it. It is a death and life situation. Christ died and rose. We have died and risen with Christ. We must therefore regard ourselves as dead to sin and alive to God.

The New Allegiance/
Wages of Sin

Questions for Thought

1. Does the Bible give a list of sins?
2. Do we need to continue in sin?
3. How can freedom in Christ be a kind of slavery?
4. Is it possible to be a genuine believer while your life remains unchanged?

Scripture says in Romans 14:23b, "And everything that does not come from faith is sin." "If anyone, then, knows the good they ought to do and doesn't do it, it is sin for them." (James 4:17). "All wrongdoing is sin, and there is sin that does not lead to death" (1John 5:17). "When he comes, he will prove the world to be in the wrong about sin and righteousness and judgment: about sin, because people do not believe in me" (John 16:8–9).

Sin pays wages (you get what you deserve), but God gives a free gift (you are given what you do not deserve).

By birth we are in Adam, the slaves of sin. By grace and faith in Christ, we are the slaves of God. Bondage to sin leads us to shame and ongoing moral decline, leading to death. Bondage to God, however, yields the precious fruit of progressive holiness, leading to the free gift of life.

It is necessary to remember who we are, on account of our conversion and our baptism. I am a new person in Christ, and by the grace of God I shall live accordingly.

God tells us repeatedly, "*My dear child, you must always remember who you are.*"

No Longer Bound to the Law

Questions for Thought

1. What is the Law?
2. Who is to blame for one's failure to come to God—the Law, sin, or me?
3. What was God's purpose in giving the Law?
4. Is the Law still binding on Christians? Are we expected to obey it?
5. Is the Law sin? Is the Law the cause of sin and death?

Those who have died to the Law are now free to belong to Christ. The Law itself is not sinful, but the purpose of the Law as a means of coming to God failed.

Through sharing in the death of Christ, the Law's curse on sin has been taken away. (Galatians 2:19, 3:10, 13) Becoming a Christian involves a drastic change of loyalty. In our old lives, we were ruled by flesh, law, sin, and death (Romans 7:5). But in our new lives, having been released from the law, we are slaves of God through the power of the Holy Spirit (Romans 7:6).

Christian freedom is freedom to serve, not freedom to sin. We are slaves of God and of righteousness. We serve not because the Law is our master and we have to but because Christ is our husband and we want to.

The Christian life is serving the risen Christ in the power of the Holy Spirit. The Law does not create sin and death; on the contrary, it is our fallen human nature that is to blame for them. The Law is cleared; sin is to blame. The Law is not to be blamed for our sins.

"Oh, how I love your law! I meditate on it all day long" (Psalm 119:97).

Struggling With Sin

Questions for Thought

1. Who is the man the apostle is describing here?
2. Is the person born again or an unbeliever?
3. Is the law sin?
4. In what way can some Christians be still slaves to rules and regulations of the Old Testament?
5. How can the Christian live in the freedom of the indwelling Holy Spirit?

The Law is God's law; it is holy, just, and good. But the Law, because of sin in man, becomes a minister of death. The Law aggravates sin (i.e., produces it). In a sense the Law makes a man sin and so brings out the "exceeding sinfulness of sin."

Unbelievers are hostile to God's law and refuse to submit to it. Believers used to be slaves of sin but now have been set free from sin and have become slaves of God and righteousness.

Old Testament Christians could be those who show signs of new birth in their love for the church and the Bible, yet their religion is law, not gospel; flesh, not Spirit. They express the "oldness" of slavery to rules and regulations, not the "newness" of freedom through Jesus Christ.

God's purpose is *not* that we should be Old Testament Christians, born again indeed but living in slavery to the Law and in bondage to indwelling sin. It is rather that we should be New Testament Christians who, having died and been raised with Christ, are living in the freedom of the indwelling Spirit.

The conquering of the sin principle could not be achieved in a day. Our only hope is in Christ for deliverance from all kinds of spiritual struggle.

The Victorious Man

Questions for Thought

1. What is walking according to the Spirit and walking according to the flesh?
2. See verse 9. Are there Christians (believers) who do not have the Spirit of God living in them?
3. How can one know that one is a child of God?
4. See verse 13. What does it mean to put to death the deeds of the sinful nature?

The indwelling Holy Spirit is both our liberator now from "the law of sin and death" (Romans 8:2) and the guarantee of resurrection and eternal glory in the end (Romans 8:11, 17, 23).

A believer is a man who is free from sin and its effects because Jesus Christ has dealt with his sin. The Christian knows by the Holy Spirit living in him that he or she is God's child. "Therefore, there is now no condemnation for those who are in Christ Jesus, because through Christ

Jesus the law of the Spirit who gives life has set you free from the law of sin and death" (Romans 8:1–2).

God justifies us through his Son and sanctifies us through his Spirit. Life in the Spirit is that which is vibrant, sustained, directed, and enriched by the Holy Spirit.

We are responsible for putting evil to death by the agency and power of the Holy Spirit. We have to pull it out, look at it, denounce it, or hate it for what it is (Matthew 5:29ff). Jesus expressed it as gouging out the offending eye and cutting off the offending hand or foot.

It is only by dying with Christ to sin, its penalty paid, that we rise to a new life of forgiveness and freedom.

The Glory of God's Children

Questions for Thought

1. What privileges do we have in being heirs with Christ?
2. See verse 17. Can we share Christ's glory without sharing his suffering?
3. See verse 27. So far what do we learn about the ministry of the Holy Spirit?
4. What are Christians groaning and eagerly waiting for?

The Christian knows by the indwelling Holy Spirit that he is God's child. All human beings are God's "offspring" by creation (Acts 17:28). But we become his reconciled children only by adoption or new birth (John 1:12, Gal. 3:26, 1 John 3:1, 10).

The Holy Spirit has liberated us from the bondage to the law and empowers us to fulfill its requirements. We live each day according to the Holy Spirit and set our minds on his desires. He lives in us and gives life to our spirit.

The Holy Spirit will one day give life to our bodies. His indwelling obliges us to live his way. His power enables us to put to death our body's misdeeds. He leads us as God's children and bears witness to our spirits that this is what we are. He is also the foretaste of our inheritance in glory.

Suffering and glory are attached to each other since suffering is the way to glory. The Christian is caught in the tension between what God has initiated (by giving us his Spirit) and what he will complete in our final adoption and redemption. We wait patiently, for we are confident in God's promises that the first fruits will be followed by the harvest, bondage by freedom, decay by that which does not decay, and labor pains by the birth of the new world.

It is a great comfort for believers to know that the Holy Spirit's intercession is effective even when our requests cannot be expressed in words.

We Are More than Super-Conquerors

Questions for Thought

1. What is predestination?
2. Has everything worked for good for you in your life?
3. See verse 31. If God is for us, who can be against us?
4. How do we know that God loves us and is for us?

Whatever the circumstances, the believer should be convinced that the course of events is for his good. God is on our side. He gave his Son for us. He justifies us. He has provided an intercessor on our behalf. He loves us. All kinds of hazards are wholly incapable of driving a wedge between the believer and God.

No one and nothing can harm the people God has foreknown, predestined, called, justified, and glorified. All the powers of hell may set themselves together against us, but they can never prevail, since God is on our side. Nothing can divide the child of God from his Father. We rejoice because all things are working together for our good. God will certainly bring us to glory. God is for us. God will not hold back anything from us. We are not condemned, and God greatly loves his people.

Life, death, fears, demonic forces, and countless other trials and circumstances attack us. But they cannot separate us from God's love or stop us from going to heaven. The Christian is no battered and exhausted victor but a confident, triumphant conqueror (Deuteronomy 29:29).

Israel's Fall

Questions for Thought

1. Has God's promise to Israel failed?
2. What is the doctrine of election?
3. Is God unfair?
4. See verses 30–33. Why do people stumble over the cross?

The Jews found a crucified Messiah to be a great obstacle that many could not accept. The law of Moses provided the pattern of achieving righteousness but gave no power to achieve it.

God brought Christ down (the incarnation) and raised him from the dead. God did it all. All that is now necessary is to confess faith in what God has done and in the lordship of Christ. These simple conditions can be fulfilled equally by Jew and Gentile. Our salvation is due entirely to his grace, will, initiative, wisdom, and power.

Israel has the adoption, divine glory, covenants, receiving the law, the temple worship, the promises, and the patriarchs, and above all from them is traced the human ancestry of Christ.

The rejected brothers Ishmael and Esau were both circumcised, and therefore in some sense they too were members of God's covenant. They were both promised lesser blessings.

God's promise did not fail. The inclusion of the Gentiles in the kingdom is a marvelous expression of God's mercy. The outsiders have been welcomed inside, the aliens have become citizens, and the strangers are beloved members of the family. "Not to us, LORD, not to us but to your name be the glory, because of your love and faithfulness" (Psalm 115:1).

Israel's Fault

Questions for Thought

1. What is necessary to salvation?
2. How do we call on the Lord?
3. What is the role of the evangelist?
4. Why then have the Israelites not believed in Jesus?

The Law as the way of getting right with God has been terminated in Christ. The reason Christ has terminated the Law is so there may be righteousness for everyone who believes. If righteousness is by the Law, it is not by Christ. If it is by Christ through faith, it is not by the Law.

The good news is that Jesus Christ died, was raised, was exalted, and now reigns as Lord. He bestows salvation on those who believe. Christ is not only easily accessible but also equally accessible to all. There is no favoritism in his ways.

To call on the name of the Lord is to appeal to him to save us in accordance with who he is and what he has done.

For one to be saved there has to be proclamation of the apostolic gospel. This is the word of faith that makes the historic Jesus Christ known. He is the incarnate, crucified, risen, reigning, and accessible Lord. Simple trust on the part of the hearers, calling on the name of the Lord by combining faith in the heart, and confession with the mouth leads to salvation.

God's initiative to Israel is even more evident. He actively holds out his hands to them (Romans 10:20–21).

God's Solution to Israel's Problem

Questions for Thought

1. Does it mean every single Israelite will be saved?
2. See verse 11. Did the Israelites stumble so as to fall beyond recovery?
3. See verses 16–18. Who are the cultivated olive tree, the root, the broken-off branches, and the wild olive shoot?
4. What warning is given to believing Gentiles?

Paul sees that all has not been lost, for Gentiles have come in where majority of Israel have stayed out. He hopes this will stir the Jews to jealousy and cause them also to come in.

Israel is thought of as an olive tree and the Gentiles as a wild shoot that has been grafted onto the original stock. Paul warns the Gentiles not to boast about this, since the branches are dependent upon the stock. In the long run they depend on God's kindness. If God can make wild olive branches productive, he can certainly restore the original tree.

God has no need to revise his promises. What he has said is unchangeable. He is unchangeable. God shows mercy to all, and the Jews are certainly not excluded.

The salvation of the Gentiles could provoke the Israelites to envy and thus lead some to conversion. The warning is that since the natural branches were broken off, the wild ones could be broken off too (Romans 11:21). The Gentiles could be rejected like the Jews. There is no room for complacency.

The promise is that since the wild branches were grafted in, the natural ones could be grafted in too (Romans 11:24). The Jews could be accepted like the Gentiles. There is no need for despair.

Our Worship of God

Questions for Thought

1. Has God rejected his people? On what grounds has God not rejected his people?
2. See verse 29. What do you understand by "for God's gifts and his call are irrevocable"?
3. Why is human pride offensive?

While Israel remains hardened, and continues to reject Christ, the gospel will be preached throughout the world. More and more Gentiles will hear it and respond to it. Meanwhile there will be a steady flow of Jews into the church, by the grace of God through faith.

In relation to election and for the sake of the patriarchs, God loves the Jews and is determined to bring them to salvation. God never goes back on his call or gifts (Romans 11:29).

Paul comes to the conclusion that God's judgments are untraceable and His ways inscrutable. Everything originates from him and exists by his permission and for his benefit.

Evangelism: (Romans 10:15) This is necessary because until people hear and receive the gospel, they are lost. The whole human race must be given the chance to hear the gospel. We must share the good news with love. Evangelists must be sent out so that the blessings that come on converts will arouse envy in others. Evangelism has hope of success only if it rests on the election of God. Converts are introduced into the people of God and so bring glory to God.

There is no room for boasting, only for humble, grateful, and wondering adoration.

To him be glory forever. Amen.

A Living Sacrifice to God

Questions for Thought

1. What is a living sacrifice?
2. See verse 21. How do you conquer evil someone has done to you by doing good?
3. See verse 20. Who are our enemies?
4. See verse 18. As Christians, is it always possible to live at peace with everybody?

A constant danger in any community of Christians is pride—some regarding themselves as more important than others. If vengeance belongs to God, then it is not necessary for a Christian to retaliate.

We should offer our bodies not to sin as instruments of wickedness but to God as instruments of righteousness. Our feet should walk his paths, our lips speak the truth and spread the gospel, and our tongues bring healing. Our hands should lift up those who have fallen, our arms embrace the lonely and unloved, our ears listen to the cries of the distressed, and our eyes look humbly and patiently toward God.

The stages of Christian moral transformation are the renewal of our minds by the Word and Spirit of God, being able then to discern and desire the will of God, and being increasingly transformed by it.

Retaliation and revenge are absolutely forbidden to the followers of Jesus.

Respect for Authority

Questions for Thought

1. What should a Christian do if demands of the state clash with his or her conscience?
2. Are Christians encouraged to show love to wicked neighbors?
3. Are there some laws that are not evil in themselves but Christians do disobey them in God's will?
4. How important is time for the Christian?

Christians have no need to be afraid of the establishment unless they do wrong. The Christian is expected to show love to his neighbor whatever the neighbor's character may be like. If we truly love our neighbors, we will seek their good, not their harm, and we will fulfill the law.

If the state commands what God forbids, or forbids what God commands, then our plain duty is to resist, not to submit, to disobey the state in order to obey God (Acts 5:29). The gospel is equally hostile to tyranny and anarchy.

The punishment of evil is God's choice, and during the present age he exercises it through the law courts. Life sentences are preferred by Christians to the death penalty because of the risk of executing innocent persons in error.

It is not Christlikeness only that we are to assume but Christ himself, laying hold of him and living under him as Lord. The self-centered flesh is still there when we put on Christ, *but* we are not to think about how to gratify its desires. We are not to make any provision for them but rather to be ruthless in putting them to death.

The Danger of Criticism

Questions for Thought

1. How does one do everything for the Lord's honor?
2. What is the spirit of criticism?
3. What does it mean to walk in love?
4. Who is a weak Christian? And who is a strong Christian?
5. How do we educate our consciences?

Paul points out the simple and basic principle that God welcomes the weak. Everything that is done should be done for the Lord's honor. If a brother feels strongly about a thing, it would be provocative for another to condemn him for it.

Paul commends that Christians should walk in love, which means consideration must be given to anyone else for whom Christ died. This means that at times some who see nothing wrong in a practice will refrain from it for the sake of the weaker brother.

A weaker brother or sister is not a vulnerable Christian who is easily overcome by temptation but a sensitive Christian full of indecision and scruples. What the weak lack is not strength of self-control but a liberty of conscience.

Stronger Christians should not be allowed to despise, browbeat, condemn, or damage weak Christians. We should welcome the weak into our fellowship, into our hearts. We should show the warmth and kindness of genuine love. We must respect the opinions of weaker brothers and sisters.

Living to Please Others

Questions for Thought

1. See verse 2. What is meant by pleasing your neighbor?
2. What concerns did Paul have as he was about to visit Judaea?
3. See verses 30–32. How do we pray in the will of God?
4. What is the prayer of petition?

The strong Christian ought to bear with the failings of the weak. They are not to please themselves. We ought not to use our strength to serve our own advantage.

Paul was essentially a pioneer. The spread of the gospel owes much to those who share the same spirit. Paul was always on the lookout for new fields in which to sow the seed of the gospel. He conceived the idea of going to Spain.

Paul is about to depart for Jerusalem with his collection fund, contributed by Christians in both Macedonia and Achaia. This was designed to alleviate the distress of the Jewish churches of Judaea and was also seen as a token of Gentile-Jewish concern.

Paul wanted the Romans to pray for him. He was uncertain what the Jewish believers would think of his collection proposal. Even Jewish Christians still shared the characteristic pride in their nation, and to accept help from Gentiles was none too easy.

We should please our neighbors and not ourselves because Christ did not please himself, because Christ is the way to united worship (Romans 15:5–6), because Christ accepted you. (Romans 15:7), and because Christ has become a servant (Romans 15:8–13).

Paul's ministry was a priestly, powerful ministry. It was a pioneer ministry.

Paul Greets His Friends

Questions for Thought

1. What made Phoebe worthy of commendation by Paul?
2. What is most interesting about the church diversity in Rome?
3. See verses 17–20. How were they to enjoy peace and crush Satan at the same time?
4. See verses 25–27. What is the scheme outlined here for making the gospel known?
5. Do we learn anything here about women in ministry?

In his testimonial for Phoebe, Paul asked the Roman church to receive her, giving her a worthy Christian welcome, and to give her any help she may need as a stranger in the capital city, presumably in connection with her other business.

Paul unexpectedly warned about false teachers who deceive and generally urged them to be on their guard.

Their enemy Satan would then deserve no better fate than to be crushed underfoot.

The theme of the letter to the Romans has been the mystery once hidden but now revealed. The most interesting and instructive aspect of the church diversity in Rome is that of gender. Nine out the twenty-six persons greeted are women.

Paul pleaded for vigilance and called for separation from those who deliberately departed from the apostolic faith. He also urged the Romans to grow in discernment.

God's peace allows no appeasement of the Devil. It is only through the destruction of evil that true peace can be attained. God's redeemed people will spend eternity ascribing to him "praise and glory and wisdom and thanks and honor and power and strength." They will worship him for his power and wisdom displayed in salvation. Amen!